Mesbah Educational Project

Share this journal with your friends!

SCAN ME

Designed by Mona Jaber

Copyright © 2023 Mona Jaber

All rights reserved.

To request permission, contact publisher at mesbahkids@gmail.com

This page is intentionally left blank.

MY RAMADAN JOURNAL

This Journal Belongs To:

Year:

This page is intentionally left blank.

DAILY PRAYERS NUMBER OF RAKAAT

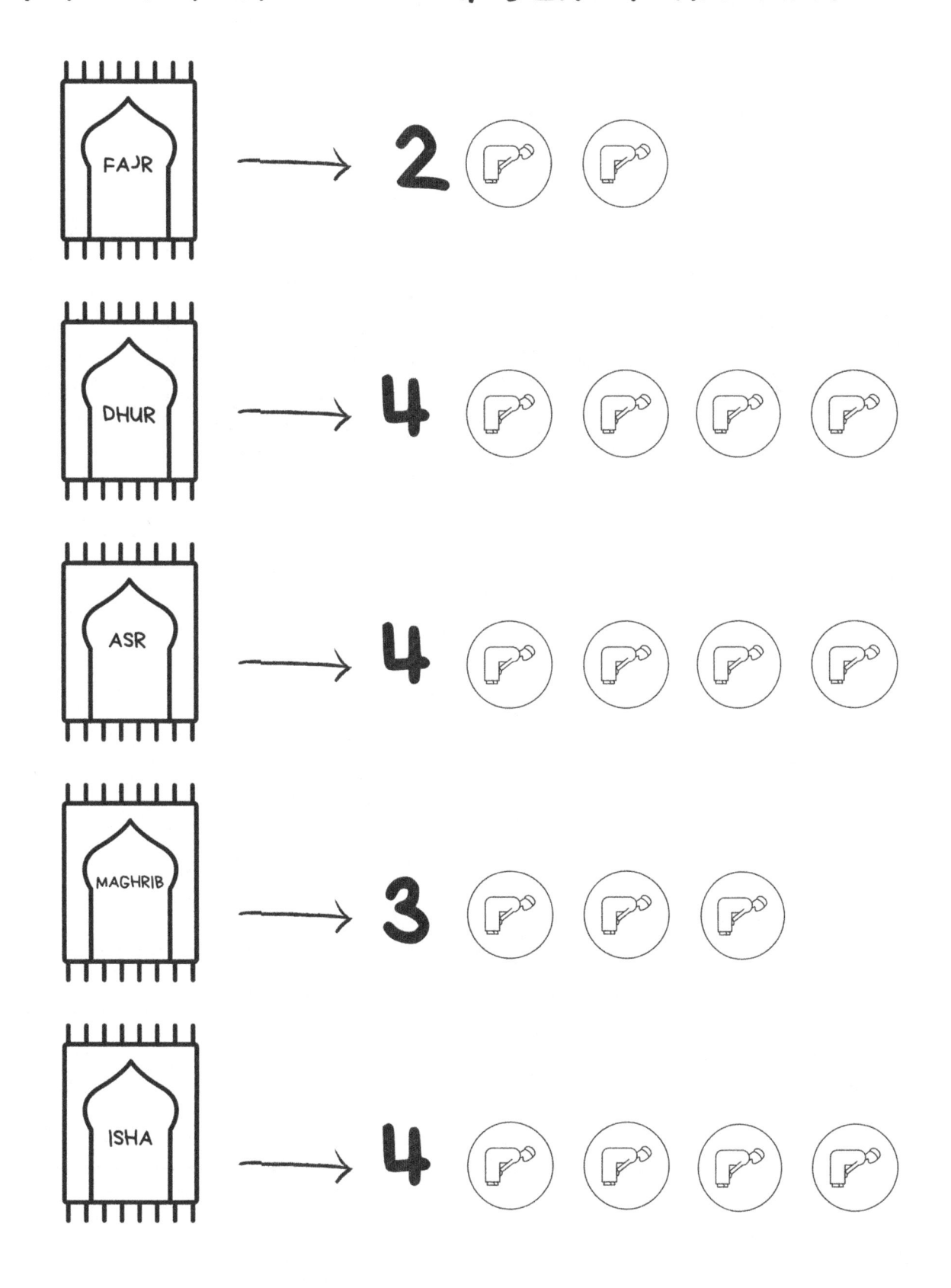

FAJR → 2

DHUR → 4

ASR → 4

MAGHRIB → 3

ISHA → 4

Mesbah Educational Project

Ramadan 1st

DATE: _____

Color a flag for every salah you performed today.

Fajr Duhr Asr Maghrib Isha

Color a medal for your fast today.

Part fast   Half fast   Most fast   Full fast

What surah did you read today? _____

Quraan reflection:

_____

_____

Mesbah Educational Project

Ramadan 1st

What good deed have you done today?

_____

_____

Color how many cups of water you drank today.

How did you feel today?

Hadith of the day:

> The Prophet (Peace Be Upon Him) said:
> "The reward of deeds depends upon the intentions and every person will get the reward according to what he has intended..."
> Sahih al-Bukhari

Ramadan 2nd

DATE: _____

Color a flag for every salah you performed today.

Fajr · Duhr · Asr · Maghrib · Isha

Color a medal for your fast today.

Part fast · Half fast · Most fast · Full fast

What surah did you read today? _____

Quraan reflection:

_____

_____

Mesbah Educational Project

Ramadan 2nd

What good deed have you done today?

_____

_____

Color how many cups of water you drank today.

How did you feel today?

Hadith of the day:

> The Prophet (Peace Be Upon Him) said:
> "When the month of Ramadan starts, the gates of the Heaven are opened, and the gates of the Hell are closed, and the devils are chained."
> Sahih al-Bukhari

Ramadan 3rd

DATE: _____

Color a flag for every salah you performed today.

Fajr Duhr Asr Maghrib Isha

Color a medal for your fast today.

Part fast   Half fast   Most fast   Full fast

What surah did you read today? _____

Quraan reflection:

_____

_____

Mesbah Educational Project

Ramadan 3rd

What good deed have you done today?

_____

_____

Color how many cups of water you drank today.

How did you feel today?

Hadith of the day:

> The Prophet (Peace Be Upon Him) said:
> "Eat Suhur (predawn meal). Surely, there is a blessing in Suhur."
> Al-Bukhari and Muslim

Ramadan 4th

DATE: _____

Color a flag for every salah you performed today.

Flags: Fajr, Duhr, Asr, Maghrib, Isha

Color a medal for your fast today.

Medals: Part fast, Half fast, Most fast, Full fast

What surah did you read today? _____

Quraan reflection:

_____

_____

Mesbah Educational Project

Ramadan 4th

What good deed have you done today?

_____

_____

Color how many cups of water you drank today.

How did you feel today?

Hadith of the day:

> The Prophet (Peace Be Upon Him) said:
> "Whoever eats or drinks forgetfully while he is fasting, let him complete his fast for Allah has fed him and given him drink."
> Sahih al-Bukhari

Ramadan 5th

DATE: _____

Color a flag for every salah you performed today.

Fajr   Duhr   Asr   Maghrib   Isha

Color a medal for your fast today.

Part fast   Half fast   Most fast   Full fast

What surah did you read today? _____

Quraan reflection:

_____

_____

Mesbah Educational Project

Ramadan 5th

What good deed have you done today?

_____

_____

Color how many cups of water you drank today.

How did you feel today?

Hadith of the day:

> The Prophet (Peace Be Upon Him) said:
> "The reward of deeds depends upon the intentions and every person will get the reward according to what he has intended..."
> Sahih al-Bukhari

Ramadan 6th

DATE: _____

Color a flag for every salah you performed today.

Fajr · Duhr · Asr · Maghrib · Isha

Color a medal for your fast today.

Part fast · Half fast · Most fast · Full fast

What surah did you read today? _____

Quraan reflection:

_____

_____

Mesbah Educational Project

Ramadan 6th

What good deed have you done today?

_____

_____

Color how many cups of water you drank today.

How did you feel today?

Hadith of the day:

The Prophet (Peace Be Upon Him) said:
"Verily, there is a gate in Paradise called al-Rayyan, through which only those who fasted will enter on the Day of Resurrection. No one else will enter it along with them.."
Al-Bukhari and Muslim

Ramadan 7th

DATE: _____

Color a flag for every salah you performed today.

Fajr Duhr Asr Maghrib Isha

Color a medal for your fast today.

Part fast   Half fast   Most fast   Full fast

What surah did you read today? _____

Quraan reflection:

_____

_____

Mesbah Educational Project

Ramadan 7th

What good deed have you done today?

_____

_____

Color how many cups of water you drank today.

How did you feel today?

Hadith of the day:

> The Prophet (Peace Be Upon Him) said: "Whoever observes fasts during the month of Ramadan out of sincere faith, and hoping to attain Allah's rewards, then all his past sins will be forgiven."
> Al-Bukhari and Muslim

Ramadan 8th

DATE: _____

Color a flag for every salah you performed today.

Fajr Duhr Asr Maghrib Isha

Color a medal for your fast today.

Part fast   Half fast   Most fast   Full fast

What surah did you read today? _____

Quraan reflection:

_____

_____

Mesbah Educational Project

Ramadan 8th

What good deed have you done today?

_____

_____

Color how many cups of water you drank today.

How did you feel today?

Hadith of the day:

The Prophet (Peace Be Upon Him) said: "Whenever you sight the new moon (of the month of Ramadan) observe fast. and when you sight it (the new moon of Shawwal) break it, and if the sky is cloudy for you, then observe fast for thirty days."
Al-Bukhari and Muslim

Ramadan 9th

DATE: _____

Color a flag for every salah you performed today.

Fajr Duhr Asr Maghrib Isha

Color a medal for your fast today.

Part fast   Half fast   Most fast   Full fast

What surah did you read today? _____

Quraan reflection:

_____

_____

Mesbah Educational Project

Ramadan 9th

What good deed have you done today?

_____

_____

Color how many cups of water you drank today.

How did you feel today?

Hadith of the day:

The Prophet (Peace Be Upon Him) said: "There is no slave of Allah who observes fasting for one day in the way of Allah, except that Allah will detach his face from hell-fire to the extent of a distance to be covered in seventy years."
Al-Bukhari and Muslim

Ramadan 10th

DATE: _____

Color a flag for every salah you performed today.

Fajr Duhr Asr Maghrib Isha

Color a medal for your fast today.

Part fast   Half fast   Most fast   Full fast

What surah did you read today? _____

Quraan reflection:

_____

_____

Mesbah Educational Project

Ramadan 10th

What good deed have you done today?

_____

_____

Color how many cups of water you drank today.

How did you feel today?

Hadith of the day:

> The Prophet (Peace Be Upon Him) said: "The difference between our observance of Sawm (fasting) and that of the people of the Scriptures is Sahur (predawn meal in Ramadan)." Muslim

Ramadan 11th

DATE: _____

Color a flag for every salah you performed today.

Fajr   Duhr   Asr   Maghrib   Isha

Color a medal for your fast today.

Part fast   Half fast   Most fast   Full fast

What surah did you read today? _____

Quraan reflection:

_____

_____

Mesbah Educational Project

Ramadan 11th

What good deed have you done today?

_____

_____

Color how many cups of water you drank today.

How did you feel today?

Hadith of the day:

> The Prophet (Peace Be Upon Him) said: "People will continue to adhere to good as long as they hasten to break the Saum (fasting)."
> Al-Bukhari and Muslim

Ramadan 12th

DATE: _____

Color a flag for every salah you performed today.

Fajr Duhr Asr Maghrib Isha

Color a medal for your fast today.

Part fast   Half fast   Most fast   Full fast

What surah did you read today? _____

Quraan reflection:

_____

_____

Mesbah Educational Project

Ramadan 12th

What good deed have you done today?

_____

_____

Color how many cups of water you drank today.

How did you feel today?

Hadith of the day:

> The Prophet (Peace Be Upon Him) said: "Allah the Most High says: 'From amongst my slaves, the quicker the one is in breaking the Saum (fasting), the dearer is he to me."
> At-Tirmidhi

Ramadan 13th

DATE: _____

Color a flag for every salah you performed today.

Fajr Duhr Asr Maghrib Isha

Color a medal for your fast today.

Part fast   Half fast   Most fast   Full fast

What surah did you read today? _____

Quraan reflection:

_____

_____

Mesbah Educational Project

Ramadan 13th

What good deed have you done today?

_____

_____

Color how many cups of water you drank today.

How did you feel today?

Hadith of the day:

"The Messenger of Allah (Peace Be Upon Him) would break the fast with fresh dates before performing Salat. If there were no fresh dates then (he would break the fast) with dried dates, and if there were no dried dates then he would take a few sips of water. At-Tirmidhi

Ramadan 14th

DATE: _____

Color a flag for every salah you performed today.

Fajr — Duhr — Asr — Maghrib — Isha

Color a medal for your fast today.

Part fast — Half fast — Most fast — Full fast

What surah did you read today? _____

Quraan reflection:

_____

_____

Mesbah Educational Project

Ramadan 14th

What good deed have you done today?

_____

_____

Color how many cups of water you drank today.

How did you feel today?

Hadith of the day:

> The Prophet (Peace Be Upon Him) said: "Whoever prayed at night the whole month of Ramadan out of sincere Faith and hoping for a reward from Allah, then all his previous sins will be forgiven.."
> Sahih al-Bukhari

Ramadan 15th

DATE: _____

Color a flag for every salah you performed today.

Fajr — Duhr — Asr — Maghrib — Isha

Color a medal for your fast today.

Part fast — Half fast — Most fast — Full fast

What surah did you read today? _____

Quraan reflection:

_____

_____

Mesbah Educational Project

Ramadan 15th

What good deed have you done today?

_____

_____

Color how many cups of water you drank today.

How did you feel today?

Hadith of the day:

> The Prophet (Peace Be Upon Him) said: "The most beloved people to Allah are those who are most beneficial to people. The most beloved deed to Allah is to make a Muslim happy, or to remove one of his troubles, or to forgive his debt, or to feed his hunger..."
> Sahih Muslim

Ramadan 16th

DATE: _____

Color a flag for every salah you performed today.

Fajr   Duhr   Asr   Maghrib   Isha

Color a medal for your fast today.

Part fast   Half fast   Most fast   Full fast

What surah did you read today? _____

Quraan reflection:

_____

_____

Mesbah Educational Project

Ramadan 16th

What good deed have you done today?

_____

_____

Color how many cups of water you drank today.

How did you feel today?

Hadith of the day:

The Prophet (Peace Be Upon Him) said: "He who feeds a fasting person will earn the same reward as him (the fasting person), without diminishing anything from the reward of the fasting person."
At-Tirmidhi

Ramadan 17th

DATE: _____

Color a flag for every salah you performed today.

Fajr · Duhr · Asr · Maghrib · Isha

Color a medal for your fast today.

Part fast · Half fast · Most fast · Full fast

What surah did you read today? _____

Quraan reflection:

_____

_____

Mesbah Educational Project

Ramadan 17th

What good deed have you done today?

_____

_____

Color how many cups of water you drank today.

How did you feel today?

Hadith of the day:

> The Prophet (Peace Be Upon Him) said: "When one of you breaks his fast, let him break it with dates for they are blessed. If they are not found, let him break it with water for it is pure."
> At-Tirmidhi

Ramadan 18th

DATE: _____

Color a flag for every salah you performed today.

Fajr Duhr Asr Maghrib Isha

Color a medal for your fast today.

Part fast   Half fast   Most fast   Full fast

What surah did you read today? _____

Quraan reflection:

_____

_____

Mesbah Educational Project

Ramadan 18th

What good deed have you done today?

_____

_____

Color how many cups of water you drank today.

How did you feel today?

Hadith of the day:

The Prophet (Peace Be Upon Him) said: "If one of you starts his day fasting, let him not engage in any obscene or ignorant speech, and if someone insults him or argues with him, let him say: I am fasting, I am fasting'"
Sahih Muslim and Bukhari

Ramadan 19th

DATE: _____

Color a flag for every salah you performed today.

Fajr Duhr Asr Maghrib Isha

Color a medal for your fast today.

Part fast   Half fast   Most fast   Full fast

What surah did you read today? _____

Quraan reflection:

_____

_____

Mesbah Educational Project

Ramadan 19th

What good deed have you done today?

_____

_____

Color how many cups of water you drink today.

How did you feel today?

Hadith of the day:

> The Prophet (Peace Be Upon Him) said: "Look for the Night of Qadr in the last ten nights of Ramadan, on the night when nine or seven or five nights remain out of the last ten nights of Ramadan (i.e. 21, 23, 25, respectively)"
> Sahih al-Bukhari

Ramadan 20th

DATE: _____

Color a flag for every salah you performed today.

Fajr · Duhr · Asr · Maghrib · Isha

Color a medal for your fast today.

Part fast · Half fast · Most fast · Full fast

What surah did you read today? _____

Quraan reflection:

_____

_____

Mesbah Educational Project

Ramadan 20th

What good deed have you done today?

_____

_____

Color how many cups of water you drank today.

How did you feel today?

Hadith of the day:

> When the last ten nights of Ramadan arrived, the Prophet (Peace Be Upon Him), peace and blessings be upon him, would tighten his belt, spend the night in worship, and awaken his family.
> Sahih al-Bukhari

Ramadan 21st

DATE: _____

Color a flag for every salah you performed today.

Fajr · Duhr · Asr · Maghrib · Isha

Color a medal for your fast today.

Part fast · Half fast · Most fast · Full fast

What surah did you read today? _____

Quraan reflection:

_____

_____

Mesbah Educational Project

Ramadan 21st

What good deed have you done today?
_____

_____

Color how many cups of water you drank today.

How did you feel today?

Hadith of the day:

The Prophet (Peace Be Upon Him) said: ""Fasting is a shield. So the fasting person should avoid obscene speech and should not behave foolishly and ignorantly, and if somebody fights with him or insults him, he should tell him twice, 'I am fasting..''
Sahih Muslim

Ramadan 22nd

DATE: _____

Color a flag for every salah you performed today.

Fajr   Duhr   Asr   Maghrib   Isha

Color a medal for your fast today.

Part fast   Half fast   Most fast   Full fast

What surah did you read today? _____

Quraan reflection:

_____

_____

Mesbah Educational Project

Ramadan 22nd

What good deed have you done today?

_____

_____

Color how many cups of water you drank today.

How did you feel today?

Hadeeth of the day:

> The Prophet (Peace Be Upon Him) said: "By the One in Whose hand is my soul, the smell that comes from the mouth of a fasting person is better in the sight of Allah than the scent of musk. (Allaah says about the fasting person)"
> Al-Bukhari and Muslim

Ramadan 23rd

DATE: _____

Color a flag for every salah you performed today.

Fajr — Duhr — Asr — Maghrib — Isha

Color a medal for your fast today.

Part fast — Half fast — Most fast — Full fast

What surah did you read today? _____

Quraan reflection:

_____

_____

Mesbah Educational Project

Ramadan 23rd

What good deed have you done today?

_____

_____

Color how many cups of water you drank today.

How did you feel today?

Hadith of the day:

> The Prophet (Peace Be Upon Him) said: "There are two joys for the fasting person: the joy when he breaks his fast, and the joy of when he meets his Lord."."
> At-Tirmidhi

Ramadan 24th

DATE: _____

Color a flag for every salah you performed today.

Fajr · Duhr · Asr · Maghrib · Isha

Color a medal for your fast today.

Part fast · Half fast · Most fast · Full fast

What surah did you read today? _____

Quraan reflection:

_____

_____

Mesbah Educational Project

Ramadan 24th

What good deed have you done today?

_____

_____

Color how many cups of water you drank today.

How did you feel today?

"Laylat Al Qadr is a night better than a thousand months"
Surah Al-Qadr

Mesbah Educational Project

Ramadan 25th

DATE: _____

Color a flag for every salah you performed today.

Fajr   Duhr   Asr   Maghrib   Isha

Color a medal for your fast today.

Part fast   Half fast   Most fast   Full fast

What surah did you read today? _____

Quraan reflection:

_____

_____

Mesbah Educational Project

Ramadan 25th

What good deed have you done today?
_____

_____

Color how many cups of water you drank today.

How did you feel today?

Hadith of the day:
> The Prophet (Peace Be Upon Him) said: "Whosoever performs Qiyam during Lailat-ul-Qadr (Night of Decree), with Faith and being hopeful of Allah's reward, will have his former sins forgiven."
> Al-Bukhari and Muslim

Ramadan 26th

DATE: _____

Color a flag for every salah you performed today.

Fajr Duhr Asr Maghrib Isha

Color a medal for your fast today.

Part fast   Half fast   Most fast   Full fast

What surah did you read today? _____

Quraan reflection:

_____

_____

Mesbah Educational Project

Ramadan 26th

What good deed have you done today?

_____

_____

Color how many cups of water you drank today.

How did you feel today?

Hadith of the day:

> "The Messenger of Allah (Peace Be Upon Him) used to strive more in worship during Ramadan than he strove in any other time of the year; and he would devote himself more (in the worship of Allah) in the last ten nights of Ramadan than he strove in earlier part of the month.
> Muslim

Ramadan 27th

DATE: _____

Color a flag for every salah you performed today.

Fajr Duhr Asr Maghrib Isha

Color a medal for your fast today.

Part fast   Half fast   Most fast   Full fast

What surah did you read today? _____

Quraan reflection:

_____
_____

Mesbah Educational Project

Ramadan 27th

What good deed have you done today?

_____

_____

Color how many cups of water you drank today.

How did you feel today?

Hadeeth of the day:

> Aisha asked: "Whoever died and he ought to have fasted (the missed days of Ramadan) then his guardians must fast on his behalf."
> Al-Bukhari

Ramadan 28th

DATE: _____

Color a flag for every salah you performed today.

Fajr   Duhr   Asr   Maghrib   Isha

Color a medal for your fast today.

Part fast   Half fast   Most fast   Full fast

What surah did you read today? _____

Quraan reflection:

_____

_____

Mesbah Educational Project

Ramadan 28th

What good deed have you done today?

_____

_____

Color how many cups of water you drank today.

How did you feel today?

Hadith of the day:

> The Prophet (Peace Be Upon Him) said: "Whoever fasts Ramadan then follows it with six days of Shawwal, it is as if he fasted for a lifetime."
> Sahih Muslim

Ramadan 29th

DATE: _____

Color a flag for every salah you performed today.

Fajr Duhr Asr Maghrib Isha

Color a medal for your fast today.

Part fast   Half fast   Most fast   Full fast

What surah did you read today? _____

Quraan reflection:

_____

_____

Mesbah Educational Project

Ramadan 29th

What good deed have you done today?

_____

_____

Color how many cups of water you drank today.

How did you feel today?

Hadith of the day:

> The Prophet (Peace Be Upon Him) said: "Eat Suhur (predawn meal). Surely, there is a blessing in Suhur."
> Sahih al-Bukhari

Ramadan 30th

DATE: _____

Color a flag for every salah you performed today.

Fajr Duhr Asr Maghrib Isha

Color a medal for your fast today.

Part fast Half fast Most fast Full fast

What surah did you read today? _____

Quraan reflection:

_____

_____

Mesbah Educational Project

Ramadan 30th

What good deed have you done today?

_____

_____

Color how many cups of water you drank today.

How did you feel today?

Hadith of the day:

> "Allah's Messenger (Peace Be Upon Him) never proceeded (for the prayer) on the Day of 'Id-ul-Fitr unless he had eaten some dates. Anas also narrated: The Prophet (Peace Be Upon Him) used to eat odd number of dates."
> Sahih al-Bukhari

Eid

DATE: _____

Color a flag for every salah you performed today.

Fajr   Duhr   Asr   Maghrib   Isha

Color the present if you have performed Eid prayer today.

Eid Prayer

What surah did you read today? _____

Quraan reflection:

_____

_____

Mesbah Educational Project

Eid

What good deed have you done today?

_____

_____

How did you feel today?

😀 🙂 😐 🙁 😮 😢

Hadith of the day:

"The Messenger of Allah (Peace Be Upon Him) obligated Zakat al-Fitr as purification of the fasting person from vain talk and misbehavior, as food for the poor. Whoever pays it before the Eid prayer, it is accepted as Zakat. Whoever pays it after the Eid prayer, it is part of voluntary charity"
Sunan Abi Dawud

EID GIFT!

Send us pictures of your Ramadan Journal book pages to **mesbahkids@gmail.com** by the end of the month of Ramadan to receive your Eid gift from Mesbah In Sha Allah.

Mesbah Educational Project

Made in the USA
Coppell, TX
14 January 2024